Territories of the United States

AMERICAN SAMOA

Danielle Haynes

PowerKiDS press

Published in 2025 by The Rosen Publishing Group, Inc.
2544 Clinton Street, Buffalo, NY 14224

First Edition

Editor: Therese Shea
Book Design: Rachel Rising

Photo Credits: Cover, p. 24 Peto Laszlo/Shutterstock.com; Cover, pp. 1, 3–32 boromvit tatasai/Shutterstock.com; Cover, pp. 1, 3–32 P-fotography/Shutterstock.com; Cover, pp. 1, 7, 11, 13, 17, 23, 27, 29 https://commons.wikimedia.org/wiki/File:Flag_of_American_Samoa.svg; p. 4 railway fx/Shutterstock.com; p. 5 Rainer Lesniewski/Shutterstock.com; p. 5 (bottom) Peter Hermes Furian/Shutterstock.com; p. 6 Justin Berken/Shutterstock.com; p. 7 Skyline Media/Shutterstock.com; p. 8 https://commons.wikimedia.org/wiki/File:Val_Dec_9_1991_0257Z.jpg; p. 9 Olmez/Shutterstock.com; p. 10 Beach Creatives/Shutterstock.com; pp. 11, 28 Danita Delimont/Shutterstock.com; p. 12 lego 19861111/Shutterstock.com; p. 13 BlueBarronPhoto/Shutterstock.com; p. 15 peacefoo/Shutterstock.com; p. 16 https://en.m.wikipedia.org/wiki/File:Aumua_Amata_Radewagen_congressional_photo.jpg; p. 17 Horizons WWP/Alamy Stock Photo; p. 18 Zarko Prusac/Shutterstock.com; p. 19 https://en.wikipedia.org/wiki/File:Va%27a_tele_or_%27alia_at_Mulinu%27u,_Samoa,_circa_1910.jpg; p. 20 f11photo/Shutterstock.com; p. 21 Smudge Whisker/Alamy Stock Photo; p. 22 Millenius/Shutterstock.com; p. 23 https://sw.m.wikipedia.org/wiki/Faili:Elisala.jpg; p. 25 https://en.m.wikipedia.org/wiki/File:American_Naval_Base,_Samoan_Islands.png; pp. 26, 27 National Museum of the U.S. Navy.

Library of Congress Cataloging-in-Publication Data

Names: Haynes, Danielle, author.
Title: American Samoa / Danielle Haynes.
Description: Buffalo, New York : PowerKids Press, [2025] | Series: Territories of the United States | Includes bibliographical references and index.
Identifiers: LCCN 2024001303 (print) | LCCN 2024001304 (ebook) | ISBN 9781725329034 (library binding) | ISBN 9781725329010 (paperback) | ISBN 9781725329041 (ebook)
Subjects: LCSH: American Samoa--Juvenile literature.
Classification: LCC DU819.A1 H38 2025 (print) | LCC DU819.A1 (ebook) | DDC 996.1/3--dc23/eng/20240130
LC record available at https://lccn.loc.gov/2024001303
LC ebook record available at https://lccn.loc.gov/2024001304

Manufactured in the United States of America

Some of the images in this book illustrate individuals who are models. The depictions do not imply actual situations or events.

CPSIA Compliance Information: Batch #CSPK25. For further information contact Rosen Publishing at 1-800-237-9932.

CONTENTS

Welcome to American Samoa

If you want to visit the southernmost spot in the United States, forget Florida. You won't find it in Hawaii either. You'll have to go much farther south to the U.S. territory of American Samoa. Located about 2,200 miles (3,540 km) south of Hawaii, the territory includes five islands and two coral **atolls**.

About 49,000 people live on the islands—Tutuila, Tau, Olosega, Ofu, and Aunuu—and one of the atolls, Swains Island. No people live on the second atoll, Rose Atoll. Tutuila is the largest and most populous island in American Samoa. It's home to the capital Pago Pago, which is known for its large, well-protected harbor.

Most people who live in the territory can speak both Samoan and English. So, take a trip to American Samoa and say "*talofa*"—or "hello"—to our friends down south!

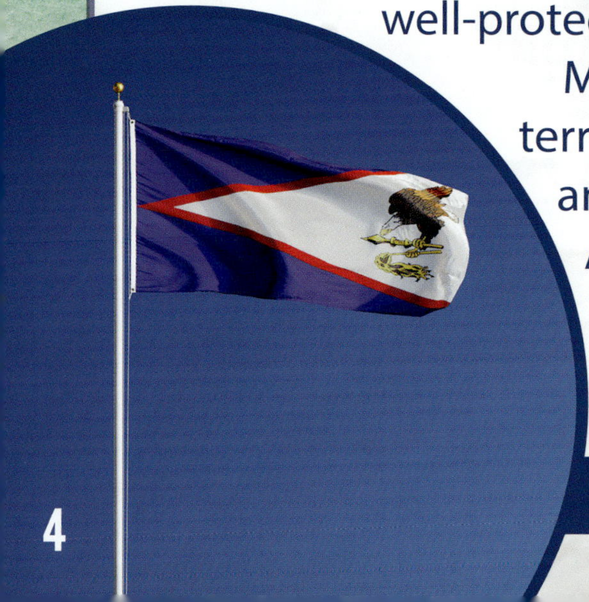

AMERICAN SAMOA FLAG

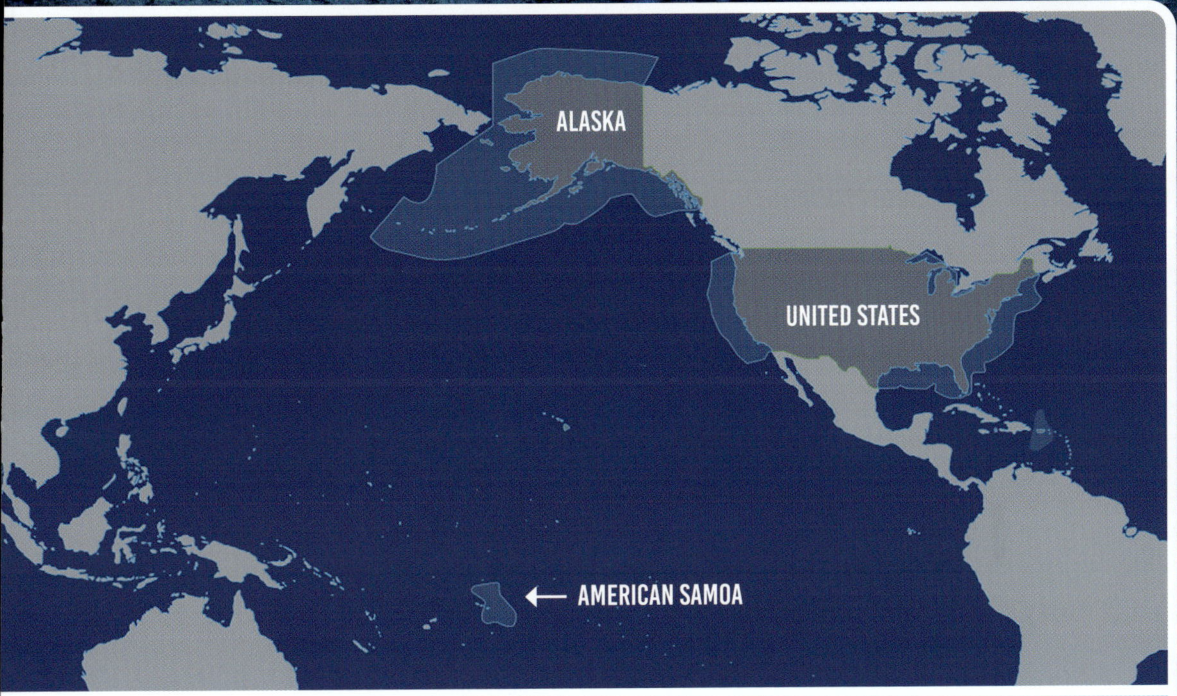

About 60 miles (97 km) separate Tutuila and Aunuu from the Manua Islands group of Ofu, Olosega, and Tau. The Rose Atoll is about 75 miles (121 km) east of the Manua Islands and Swains Island is some 350 miles (563 km) north of Tutuila.

The Samoan Archipelago

American Samoa is the eastern part of a group of several islands called an archipelago. The western part of the archipelago is the country of Samoa, formerly called Western Samoa. Together, the entire archipelago is also called Samoa.

Volcanoes formed the main islands of American Samoa starting about 7 million years ago. The atolls, however, are made of coral. Corals also form reefs around the islands, in some cases creating lagoons.

The total land area of American Samoa is about 76 square miles (197 sq km), most of which is Tutuila. The islands are covered by lush rainforests that are home to many species of birds and insects. The surrounding Pacific Ocean is also an important home for many sea creatures, including eight species of whales.

HUMPBACK WHALES

WHAT'S AN ARCHIPELAGO?

An archipelago is a chain of islands in a body of water. You can find them in oceans, lakes, and even rivers! The Samoan archipelago formed when volcanoes under the Pacific Ocean erupted, causing lava, or molten rock, to build up until it created a land mass above the water's surface. Other archipelagos are made from the buildup of coral reefs. Coral reefs form when coral larvae attach to underwater rocks or other hard places near islands or continents.

American Samoa is part of Polynesia, a group of more than 1,000 islands in the central and southern Pacific Ocean. The name "Polynesia" is formed from two Greek words: *polús*, meaning "many" and *nêsos*, meaning "island."

Weather and Climate Change

American Samoa has a tropical climate, which means it receives lots of rain and is generally hot most of the time. The city of Pago Pago gets about 200 inches (508 cm) of rain each year. The average temperature ranges from the high 60s Fahrenheit (around 20°C) to the low 90s Fahrenheit (around 30°C).

Hurricanes—often called cyclones in this part of the world—are rare in American Samoa but can be a serious threat when they happen. On average, the territory sees one cyclone per year. One storm, called Tropical Cyclone Val, brought much destruction in December 1991. Val reached wind speeds of 143 miles (230 km) per hour, killing more than a dozen people and damaging buildings and boats.

TROPICAL CYCLONE VAL

Territorial Truths ☆☆☆☆☆

Human activities—mostly the burning of fossil fuels—has caused climate change in American Samoa. This can be seen in higher air and ocean temperatures, a rise in sea level, rain pattern changes, and ocean **acidification**.

Mount Pioa, 1,716 feet (523 m) high, is also called Rainmaker Mountain because it traps rain clouds. Rain caused by mountains like this is called orographic.

Flora and Fauna

The plants and animals that naturally grow and live in American Samoa are well suited to the warm, humid, or moist, rainforest. Flora refers to the plant life of a region. In American Samoa, the plant life consists mostly of many species of evergreen trees and **ferns**.

There are about 540 native species of plants in the territory, some 186 of which can only be found there! American Samoa has the largest variety of orchid species in all of Polynesia, with more than 100 examples.

The Samoan archipelago has lost about 80 percent of its low-lying rainforests. People cleared this land of trees so it could be used to grow cash crops such as **taro** and bananas.

SWAMP ORCHID

FORESTS IN THE SKY

The entire Samoan archipelago is known for a special feature called a cloud forest. These are tropical mountainous regions in which vast humid forests of trees grow. There is often much rainfall in these forests, and they typically occur at about 3,000 to 8,000 feet (914 to 2,438 m) in altitude. As of 2022, only about 1 percent of the world's woodlands are cloud forests. This figure has fallen from 11 percent in the 1970s, mostly due to climate change and **deforestation**.

The U.S. National Park Service protects many of the plants and trees on multiple islands in American Samoa, including on Ofu, pictured above. The colorful swamp orchid, shown at left, is one of more than 100 orchids found in American Samoa.

These many trees and the vast ocean waters create plenty of homes for American Samoa's wildlife. Fauna refers to the animal life of a region. There aren't many land mammals in American Samoa, but one definitely stands out. The territory is home to flying foxes, the world's largest species of bat. They can grow to 16 inches (40 cm) in body length with a wingspan of 5 feet (1.5 m). They're important pollinators on the islands, along with bees, butterflies, and other insects.

Other land mammals include rats, mice, and pigs, while land reptiles such as geckos, skinks, and snakes also crawl and slither around. There's even the odd amphibian in the form of cane toads. Native birds include terns, boobies, frigatebirds, petrels, honeyeaters, cardinals, and Samoan starlings. Many fly to the territory just to breed.

WHITESPOTTED SURGEONFISH

FAUNA AT SEA

A huge **diversity** of fish and marine mammals also call the ocean around American Samoa home. There are more than 800 native fish species, as well as 200 coral species! Marine mammals in the area include whales (humpback, sperm, short-finned pilot, killer, and minke) and dolphins (spinner, rough-toothed, bottlenose, pantropical spotted, and striped). The U.S. government protects this important ecosystem in the Pacific Ocean at the National Marine **Sanctuary** of American Samoa.

Bats are famously nocturnal animals, meaning they're active mostly at night. But the flying foxes that live in American Samoa, *Pteropus samoensis*, like to be awake during the day.

Calling American Samoa Home

Most of the 49,000 people who live in American Samoa are **ethnically** Samoan with Polynesian ancestry. That means they share a common background with other people who have lived on the archipelago for thousands of years. In 2020, about 83 percent of people in the territory reported they were Samoan, while 3.4 percent were Filipino, 2.2 percent were Tongan, and 11.2 percent were a variety of other ethnicities.

Since Samoans are Polynesian, they share some **culture** and ways of life with other Polynesian groups in New Zealand, French Polynesia, Hawaii, and Tonga.

Most people speak both the Samoan language as well as English. About half the population is **Protestant**, 18 percent are Roman Catholic, and nearly 16 percent are Mormon as of 2015. As of 2020, 87.2 percent of people live in cities, and 12.8 percent live in rural areas.

Territorial Truths ☆☆☆☆☆

American Samoans feel strongly about preserving their culture from before the arrival of European and American explorers and colonizers. They call this Samoan way *fa'asamoa*.

American Samoans of Polynesian descent may wear cultural clothing while taking part in celebrations.

Samoan communities have a very important organizational system called *matai*. Each village is made up of multiple *aiga*, which are extended family groups. Each of these family groups is headed by a chief called a matai. The chief represents their family on the village council, called a *fono*, and has control over all the family members' wealth.

The highest chief on the fono is called the *ali'i*. Each village also includes a *pulenu'u*, who acts as a mayor or police chief, and at least one *tulafale*, a talking chief or storyteller. The tulafale has always been an important figure in Samoan culture. They tell the village's legends, stories, and histories. Before written language arrived on the islands, the storytellers passed down the only records of Samoan history for generations.

AUMUA AMATA RADEWAGEN, REPRESENTATIVE FOR AMERICAN SAMOA IN U.S. CONGRESS

WOMEN IN AMERICAN SAMOA

Samoan culture is traditionally patriarchal, meaning women mostly take care of the home and raise children while men work outside the home. Because the men provide money for the family, they also usually have the final say in most family decisions. However, some women serve as the matai for their aiga. To do so, a woman must be the daughter of an ali'i within the same aiga she is to serve as matai. Women are becoming more and more influential in Samoan culture.

A tulafale traditionally holds a type of fly swatter called a *fue* while giving speeches, seen on this Samoan's shoulder.

The First Polynesians

Human history on the Samoan archipelago dates back about 3,000 years, roughly 1000 BCE. This is a little bit after the start of the Iron Age (1050 BCE), when people first began using iron tools in many parts of the world.

Historians believe these first Polynesian settlers were from Tonga, a country made up of about 170 islands. The early Tongans used boats called outrigger canoes to travel the roughly 550 miles (885 km) to Samoa. Archaeologists found broken pieces of pottery in a lagoon in Samoa that told them the early settlers likely came from Tonga. The Samoan language and Tongan language also share similarities. Legends passed down for hundreds of years say Samoans, Tongans, and Fijians shared contact over the generations.

Territorial Truths ☆☆☆☆☆

Because they live on hundreds of islands far away from any large land masses, Polynesian culture has mostly centered around life at sea. Traditionally, Polynesians are master navigators, boatbuilders, and fishers.

Polynesians used large outrigger canoes to travel between islands hundreds of miles apart. Samoans called these boats, pictured, *'alia*, while Fijians called them *drua* and Tongans used the term *kalia*.

European Explorers

The first European to step foot on the Samoan archipelago was Dutch explorer Jacob Roggeveen. He began trading with Samoans living on the Manua Islands group in 1722. In 1830, Christian missionary John Williams, a member of the London Missionary Society, traveled to Samoa to convert Samoans to the Christian religion.

More foreigners from the United States, Great Britain, and Germany arrived on the islands throughout the 19th century, creating a foreign settlement near Apia Harbor on the Samoan island of Upolu. These explorers wanted to bring the archipelago under foreign rule. Rival matai fought among themselves in support of or against the three countries seeking control.

In the end, the United States **annexed** the area now known as American Samoa, while Germany took control of Western Samoa—now simply called Samoa.

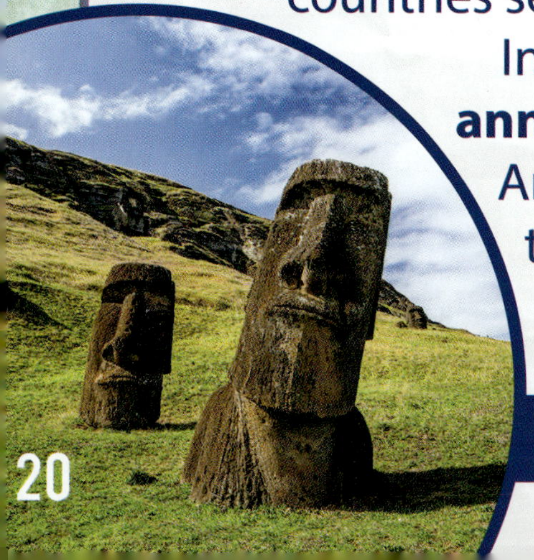

EASTER ISLAND

Territorial Truths ☆☆☆☆☆

Jacob Roggeveen set off from the Netherlands in 1721 with three ships: the *Arend*, the *Thienhoven*, and the *Afrikaansche Galey*.

Jacob Roggeveen was the first European to visit Easter Island, named because he first arrived there on the Christian holiday. There he and his crew (shown) found large stone statues called *moai*.

Becoming American Samoa

The United States didn't take control of what would become American Samoa all at once. The matai granted the island of Tutuila to the U.S. government in 1900. The Manua Islands joined in 1904 and Swains Island in 1925.

The U.S. Navy had authority over the territory until 1951. The Interior Department, the part of the U.S. government that oversees federal lands, took control in 1956. American Samoa adopted its own territorial constitution in 1967.

American Samoa is the only U.S. territory the United States doesn't grant citizenship to. They're considered nationals, not citizens. As such, they can't vote in federal elections, can't serve as officers in the U.S. military, and can't hold certain jobs, even if they live in the mainland United States.

THE LAST HOLDOUT

Not every Samoan agreed with the United States' annexation of the eastern islands. Tui Manu'a Elisara, chief of the Manua Islands, at first refused to sign the deed of **cession** to the United States. He wanted to remain in charge of his people. But in 1904, he agreed to give up control after the U.S. government withheld money to fund a school. He maintained leadership under the title "district governor" until his death in 1909.

The anniversary of the day Tui Manu'a Elisala, pictured, signed the Deed of Cession, July 16, 1904, is celebrated in American Samoa as Manua Cession Day.

The Mau Movement

Many Samoans in both Samoa and American Samoa resisted the rule of the European and American colonizers. They wanted to be in control of their own lands and lives, a concept known as self-determination. This resistance was called the Mau Movement. *Mau* means "opinion" in Samoan.

While this was primarily a Samoan uprising, the Mau Movement was also felt in American Samoa. One of its chief supporters was Samuel Ripley, who had both American and American Samoan citizenship because his grandfather was an American. Ripley primarily lived in California but traveled often to American Samoa in support of what he called "the Samoan Cause."

Supporters produced a petition accusing the U.S. government of keeping Samoans ignorant of law, poorly developing roads and schools outside of the naval base, and preventing chiefs from having meetings.

PAGO PAGO

Territorial Truths ☆☆☆☆☆

In 1926, Ripley sued U.S. Navy captain Waldo Evans, governor of the territory, for wrongfully arresting him and deporting him to California. The case brought attention to the legality of U.S. martial rule over the territory.

The U.S. Navy chose Pago Pago as the site for its military base because of its deepwater harbor. It was an active base from 1900 until the end of the navy's authority over the territory in 1951.

Going to War

American Samoa was important to the U.S. military during World War II. The territory served as a critical link between the United States and other **Allied** nations in the war, especially Australia and New Zealand.

On January 11, 1942, the territory came under fire for the only time during the entire war, by a Japanese submarine. Later that month, the U.S. Marines positioned 5,600 service members at the naval station in Pago Pago to defend the territory and trade route to Australia. A group of 350 Samoans, the 1st Samoan Battalion, Marine Corps Reserve, founded in 1941, was part of the effort.

Tutuila was also an ideal location for jungle training for service members preparing to fight in the jungles of the South Pacific.

THE BAREFOOT MARINES

Members of the Samoan battalion can be easily identified in old war photos by their uniform. The marines wore a traditional skirt-like wrap around their waist called a *lava-lava*. The Marine Corps logo was placed along the bottom. They wore a simple, white undershirt and a standard cap with a red patch. Because the battalion wore no shoes, they were known as the Barefoot Marines. Historians say shoes weren't part of Samoan culture until Europeans colonized the islands.

The U.S. Marines broke up the Samoan battalion in January 1944.

American Samoa Today

Today, life in American Samoa is fairly quiet and slower paced than in the mainland United States. Life revolves around the family, church, and village. Many families gather on Sundays for large family meals called *to'ona'i*. American Samoa has a young population compared to the greater United States, with more than half under the age of 30, compared to about 40 percent for the whole country.

The largest employer is the federal government, which provides many grants to the territory. Many people also work at tuna canning companies and in the tourism industry. Many American Samoans have earned national and global fame, including former politician Tulsi Gabbard, novelist Sia Figiel, beauty pageant winner Marion Malena, and athletes including martial artist Mighty Mo, football players Michael Iupati and Isaac Sopoaga, and rugby player Jerome Kaino.

TIMELINE

1000 BCE	Polynesians first arrive on the Samoan archipelago, likely from Tonga.
1722 CE	The first Europeans, led by Dutch explorer Jacob Roggeveen, step foot on Samoa.
1830	Christian missionary John Williams, from Britain, arrives to convert Samoans.
1900	The matai sign land grants making the island of Tutuila a U.S. territory. Pago Pago become home to a U.S. military base.
1904	The Manua Islands join the United States.
1925	The last of what would become American Samoa, Swains Island, joins the United States.
1942	Thousands of U.S. Marines are positioned at the naval station in Pago Pago during World War II.
1951	The U.S. Navy ends its authority over American Samoa.
1956	The Interior Department takes up administration over the territory.
1967	American Samoa adopts its own constitution.
1991	Tropical Cyclone Val hits the islands.

Glossary

acidification: The increase of carbon dioxide in the ocean, which in turn makes the water more acidic.

Allied: Having to do with the group of nations, including England and the United States, in World War II that opposed the Axis nations, including Germany and Japan.

annex: To take over an area and make it part of a larger territory.

atoll: A coral island that encircles a lagoon.

cession: One state yielding to another.

culture: The beliefs and ways of life of a certain group of people.

deforestation: The act or result of cutting down or burning all the trees in an area.

diversity: The quality or state of having many different types, forms, or ideas.

ethnically: Belonging to a certain group of people with a particular culture.

fern: A type of flowerless plant with leaves called fronds.

Protestant: A member of one of the Christian churches that separated from the Roman Catholic Church in the 1500s.

sanctuary: A place of protection for wildlife and plants.

taro: A type of root vegetable native to Southern India and Southeast Asia.

For More Information

Books

Changues, Yiling. *Tales of Polynesia: Folktales from Hawai'i, New Zealand, Tahiti, and Samoa.* San Francisco, CA: Chronicle Books, 2023.

Macintosh, Cameron. *Islands of the Pacific.* Victoria, Australia: Cengage Learning Australia, 2023.

Weiss, Sabrina M. *Amazing Islands: 100+ Places That Will Boggle Your Mind.* Greenbelt, MD: What on Earth Books, 2020.

Websites

American Samoa Visitors Bureau
www.americansamoa.travel
Check out the official website of the American Samoa Visitors Bureau, and learn about all the things to see and do in the territory.

Britannica: American Samoa
www.britannica.com/place/American-Samoa
Read more about the history, geography, and people of American Samoa.

National Park of American Samoa
www.nps.gov/npsa/index.htm
Visit the official website of the National Park of the American Samoa, which is home to important cultural and natural resources.

INDEX